A QUICK HISTORY OF MONEY

A QUICK HISTORY OF MONEY

FROM BARTERING TO BITCOIN

Clive Gifford and Rob Flowers

WIDE EYED EDITIONS

CONTENTS

INTRODUCTION

Cash, moolah, dough, green... Whatever you call **money**, there's a lot of it about, yet never quite enough of it in your own pocket.

Just how much money is out there? Well, there's an estimated **36,800,000,000,000** (36.8 trillion, or 36.8 thousand billion) US dollars out and about, circulating as banknotes, coins, and in easy-access bank accounts. That's just the tip of the iceberg...

Most money in the world is held electronically, stored on computers or flowing around computer networks. Trillions of dollars more are held in investments.

Money is an imaginative **HUMAN INVENTION**. It's the idea of using something with an agreed value that's accepted by people to make buying and selling easier. That "something" can be almost anything—from tea, cheese, and beads to cows, dirty great rocks, whale's teeth, and even children (those Aztecs were pretty mean).

AN ICE CREAM FOR THE KID?

SOUNDS LIKE A FAIR DEAL.

Money also makes it easier to measure and compare. It allows people to put a price or value on objects or work they carry out.

This book takes you through money's amazing journey, from mighty, moneyless empires to the pizzas worth $465 million—along the way checking out history's wealthiest individuals, how banks make money from money, and what the future might hold for money and you.

So, let's start our **tale of money** by rewinding to when there was none whatsoever.

A TIME BEFORE MONEY

Imagining life without money can lead to brain ache. Think about it for a little while. Bet all sorts of questions pop up in your head.

Well, back in the day (we're talking more than 12,000 years ago), there were no zucchinis* or computers, nor were there governments, taxes, or shops. A day out at the mall or market simply wasn't happening.

*The zucchini was developed from American squashes by gardeners in Italy only a couple of hundred years ago.

Early people lived their lives as wanderers called **NOMADS**. They roamed the land, hunting animals and birds, and gathering plants, fruits, seeds, and roots to eat.

When you don't have a home and are constantly on the move, it's funny how little stuff you need. Not much more perhaps than an animal skin to keep you warm, sharp stones to cut and scrape, and a pointy stick to hunt and defend yourself.

This style of life continued in some parts of the world to this day. Handfuls of isolated tribes, like the **AWA** in the Amazon rainforest and the **SENTINELESE** in the Indian Ocean, still hunt, gather, and live without money. Other peoples with no money prospered in the past by using **PRESENTS**.

IT'S A GIFT

We all like to receive **GIFTS**. Most of us like to give them, too. Some people in the past relied on gift-giving to cover their needs and those of others.

For instance, giving gifts of food that had been hunted or gathered that day acted like **INSURANCE**. Even skilled hunters gave, so they wouldn't stay hungry if they had a bad day at the office the next day. (And when I say office, I mean out on the plains or in forests or rivers.)

A lot of **GIFTING** did the giver good in the eyes of others, building their status and power.

Gifting may have continued long after some humans began **SETTLING** down around 10,000 years ago. Instead of wandering around, people started staying put, farming the land, and raising livestock. As a result, the amount of stuff they owned started to expand greatly.

Some tribes and peoples made gifting **COMPULSORY**. They gathered together everyone's spare crops and goods and then handed them all out. The **HAUDENOSAUNEE** Native Americans, for example, had a council of senior women who decided who got what from their crops, all stored in wooden longhouses.

Thousands of miles south, the **INCAS** went further. This mighty South American empire had no money, markets, or traders whatsoever. Instead, Inca rulers gave people work to do and supplied them with food, tools, and other basic goods like clothes. The system was called **MIT'A** and saw the hardest workers receive extra gifts as bonuses… while the laziest could look forward to a severe beating or death.

GIFTING is great, but many early people believed **BARTER** was better...

SWAP SHOP

We believe **BARTERING** began around 8,000 years ago in the Middle East and Asia. No one's certain, as details weren't written down. Why? Because writing hadn't been invented.

Imagine you are an early farmer with a bumper harvest of apples—more than you can eat. What you really want is something less apple-y, a chicken to lay eggs, perhaps.

You need to find someone who not only has spare chickens, but who also wants apples… and who wants to make a trade at the same time as you.

This is known as the **DOUBLE COINCIDENCE OF WANTS**, which didn't always happen. But if you did find someone interested, you then needed to agree a fair **RATE OF EXCHANGE** with them.

Sometimes, people might have to barter a number of times to finally get what they were after.

APPLES >> SACK OF BARLEY >> FIGS >> A CHICKEN
HURRAH!

By the way, barter's still used today whenever friends swap toys, clothes, or trading cards. It's also been used very occasionally to transfer footballers between clubs, such as when **HUGH MCLENAHAN** was transferred to Manchester United in 1927 for two freezers full of ice cream.

Barter worked best back in the distant past when there were only a few different things, known as **COMMODITIES**, to swap. As settlements grew, things got complicated. People made and wanted more and more items—from pottery and jewelry to tools and weapons. You might spend ages looking and STILL not find a bartering partner. And that wasn't the only problem…

COW MUCH?

Barter had its moments, but also its flaws. What if the thing you have to offer is worth much, **MUCH** more than the item you want? While you can split up many crops, bartering half a shirt or sword for something doesn't work—dividing such items makes them useless to both parties.

Many things early people had to swap were fresh crops with a limited life span. The pressure was on to strike a deal before the crops went off and suddenly lost their value.

Others might be up for a swap, but their own crop or livestock may still be growing and not ready yet.

To get round some of these timing problems, **IOU**s were eventually invented. These were **PLEDGES** to pay at a later date. Most early people lived all their lives in one place, so they were easily found if they didn't pay up.

An alternative was to try to own things that kept their value for a longer time. Cows lived for 15 years or more. They provided milk daily as well as meat and leather when they died.

Some people built up herds of cattle as a way to keep hold of their wealth, knowing they could exchange a cow for other things later on. The Latin word "CAPUT," meaning "head" (as in "200 head of cattle"), is also the root of the word "capital," meaning wealth and financial assets.

WHY IS FLAVIUS SLEEPING ON A COW?

HE LIKES TO KEEP HIS MONEY UNDER HIS BED.

Cows had become what we call a "STORE OF VALUE," as would other things...

ALL THAT GLITTERS

Cows had their place, but carrying cattle as cash on a long journey was a no-no. What was needed was something more portable that lots of people wanted and agreed was valuable. Precious metals like **GOLD** and **SILVER** provided an answer.

GOLD is rare enough to have value. It also stays **SHINY** and is **EASY TO SHAPE**, but not strong enough to make tools, ploughs, and swords. Early metalworkers could hammer it into thin sheets and pull it into thin threads. A single gram of gold can make a thread over a mile long. **AWESOME.**

RESEARCHERS THINK THAT ALL THE GOLD THAT HAS EVER BEEN MINED WOULD FIT INTO ROUGHLY THREE OLYMPIC SWIMMING POOLS.

>> FAST FORWARD >> to 1972 when a Bulgarian digger truck uncovered something rather wonderful near Lake Varna.

<<REWIND << It was the oldest collection of treasures made of gold— 6,200–6,600 years old.

By 3600 BCE, *Egyptian* metalworkers became skilled at melting rocky chunks to separate out the gold they contained. By 3100 BCE, there was even an early **EXCHANGE RATE** in *Egypt*: gold was worth 2½ times its weight in silver. (The rate today is more like 80 or 90 times.)

Much of the gold found in and around *Egypt* made its way into the **PHARAOH'S TREASURY**. Famous pharaoh **TUTANKHAMUN** was buried in a coffin made from 243 lbs of solid gold. That's serious moolah!

Gold would go on to power money in many places, but not everyone on the planet valued it so highly. Almost 200 years ago, a chest crammed full of gold coins washed up on the shores of **FIJI**. On these islands, gold was worth zilch. Some Fijians had fun skimming the coins like stones across the Pacific Ocean.

THEY LITERALLY THREW AWAY A FORTUNE!

SHELLING OUT

The Fijians had their own object of stored value instead of gold at the time and that was **TABUA**—the teeth of sperm whales. Some could weigh **1 KG** or **MORE**.

Many other early people also lacked gold and silver. They plumped for other items, rare in their world, as a store of value. For an object to work in this way, it needed to be durable and not perish or break easily.

Ice: great as a popsicle, rubbish as money.

Ice, of course, was never really used as money. **SEASHELLS** proved a better bet. They were **HARD** and **TOUGH**, some were rare, and many were small, such as **COWRIES**. These smooth, egg-shaped shells are found in the Pacific and Indian oceans.

COWRIES became widely used as money in **AFRICA** and parts of **ASIA**. In the Maldives, people put out mats woven from palm leaves at the water's edge, hoping cowries would congregate and make them rich.

In **CHINA**, cowries were imported from the South China Sea to be used as money inland at least 3,400 years ago. So much so, that the Chinese character for "money" comes from the symbol for the **SHELL**.

Each shell was called a bèi and a small series of shells on a string, a péng. Around 20 péngs could buy you two or three farm fields. So, when the first ever female Chinese general, Fu Hao, was buried in 1200 BCE with 6,900 bèi, we think she died with a **BIG** fortune.

LOOKS LIKE SHE REALLY LOVED SEAFOOD.

Around 1000 BCE, China began making imitation cowry shells out of bronze. However, they weren't the first to use set weights of metal as money…

MESOPOTAMIA'S GOT TALENT[S]

MESOPOTAMIA (where present-day Iraq is located) was full of smart people. More than 5,000 years ago, it was the birthplace of the **WHEEL**, **WRITING**, and the **PLOUGH**, among other super-handy things. The region was also where specific weights of metal were first used as **MONEY**.

The metal was silver and it was divided up into weight units called **SHEKELS**, **MINA**, and **TALENTS**. A shekel was about 8.4 g of silver. A regular Mesopotamian needed to graft for around 17 days straight to earn a single shekel.

There were 60 shekels to a mina and 60 minas to a talent, which equalled about 65 lbs—not far off what you weigh. It was also thought of as the maximum weight a regular adult could comfortably carry.

Barter and trading using weights of barley and other crops also occurred, but **SET WEIGHTS OF SILVER** were really useful for big purchases such as buying land—or for paying off fines for crimes.

The oldest surviving set of laws are found on clay tablets from southern Mesopotamia, made by King Ur-Nammu about 4,100 years ago. If you committed murder, Law 1 stated that you were to be put to death. Committed robbery? Death. Flooded a man's field with water? Well, you had to pay him a fine of barley, according to Law 31. **OTHER FINES INCLUDED:**

- 2 shekels for knocking out a tooth
- 10 shekels for cutting off a foot
- ⅔ mina for cutting a nose off with a copper knife

So, who did the fines go to and who was in charge of weighing and storing all the silver?

OWE NO!

We think priests in MESOPOTAMIA judged the
weight of silver and stored it for safekeeping.
Before silver, they may have looked after little
clay pouches. These contained tokens, also
made of clay—the Mesopotamians liked clay.
Many TOKENS featured a simple picture of a
cow, sheep, or another owned object.

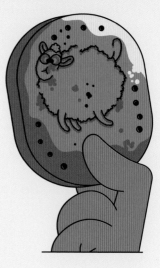

Tokens could also act as a record of what you owed, such as promising
to deliver a lamb to someone once it was born.

Some of the region's TEMPLES first became banks at least 5,000 years
ago. At the time, storing your valuables in a temple made perfect sense.
They were one of the strongest buildings around and thieves were unlikely
to steal from them for fear of offending the gods. But that didn't stop the
banks themselves from skimming a little off the top.

Today, banks often give you a little money, called **INTEREST**, for the privilege of keeping your money safe and secure. That's not a bad deal compared to the past. The earliest banks charged you as much as $\frac{1}{60}$ th of your wealth, just for looking after it.

Keeping financial records of who had what led the Sumerians from MESOPOTAMIA to develop the first ever written language. They used a reed to press shapes representing numbers into tablets made of, guess what? Yup, more clay.

Temples in MESOPOTAMIA also made the world's first bank loans, offering farmers seeds or tools (or silver to buy them) with the idea that these would be paid back after the farmer's harvest... often with interest...

VERY INTERESTING

Those seeds or tools loaned to you were rarely an act of kindness. You were expected to pay back the loan and also a little extra—called **INTEREST**.

People in **MESOPOTAMIA** developed two types of interest still used today: simple and compound. **SIMPLE INTEREST** is, er, pretty simple. The interest rate is a fraction or percentage of the amount you borrow (called the principal). So, if you borrowed 20 goats at a rate of 5%, you'd owe one extra goat as interest.

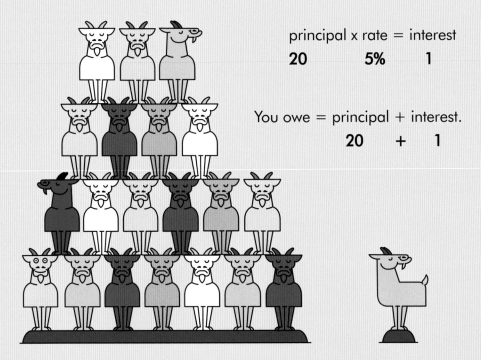

principal x rate = interest
20   5%   1

You owe = principal + interest.
          20   +   1

If you borrowed for a year at a rate of 5% each month, the **INTEREST** rate would total 60% or 12 goats. So far, so simple. Here's where it gets complicated...

COMPOUND INTEREST is interest charged on both the principal AND interest you owe. The **BABYLONIANS** called it şibāt şibtim meaning "interest on interest."

We'll save you from the math—we're good like that. But if you borrowed 20 goats for a year at 5% monthly compound interest, you'd owe not 12 but almost 16 goats plus the original 20.

Now, if you made the same two deals above, but for 20 years, under **SIMPLE INTEREST**, you'd owe a big herd (260 goats) in total.

But that's nothing compared to what you'd owe under **MONTHLY COMPOUND INTEREST**... 2,434,791 goats—just for borrowing 20. Mind-blowing, isn't it?

Wars have been fought over compound interest and its effects. The first we know about was around 2400 BCE when the cities of Umma and Lagash clashed over Umma not paying masses of barley as

COINING IT

West of warring cities in MESOPOTAMIA, a kingdom called **LYDIA** sprang up around 3,300 years ago in what is now western Turkey. Its location was crucial as trade between places around the Mediterranean Sea began to boom.

Bars of silver and gold were commonly used when traders bought and sold big. But they were not easily divided up at a port for smaller purchases. They also had to be carefully weighed and checked each time they were used, and not all traders could be trusted.

Small, sort-of-circular discs of metal were first made during the reigns of Lydia's kings, Sadyattes and Alyattes (650–560 BCE). They all weighed the same (= 240 grains of wheat), were worth the same amount, and were called STATERS. These were the world's first coins.

There were also smaller coins, called **TRITES**, that were worth one-third of a stater. **STATERS** and **TRITES** were made of **ELECTRUM**—an alloy (mixture) of gold and silver that's found naturally. It was especially found in the River Pactolus that flowed through Lydia. Now, that's handy!

We think a bit of fine-tuning of the metal content went on, so that each coin was 55% **GOLD** and 45% **SILVER**. This would mean each was the same store of value. The tiniest amount of **COPPER** was also added to the mix to help give the coins a shiny appearance.

What really made this money important was how each coin was stamped with an official design—the **LYDIAN LION**. This told people that the money was the real deal. It didn't take long for much of the ancient world to go completely coin-crazy.

COINS CATCH ON

COINS quickly became all the rage. King Alyattes' heir, Croesus, introduced the first bimetallic (two-metal) currency, with pure silver and pure gold coins called **CROESEIDS**. One gold croeseid was worth 13 silver ones. Croesus became so famous for being wealthy that even today you might hear people described as being "as rich as Croesus."

When Lydia was conquered by the Persians in 546 BCE, croeseids spread through the Persian empire. Meanwhile, in India, square pieces of silver were used as coins.

Greek city-states were desperate for easy, portable ways to pay their mercenaries (foreign soldiers). Coins proved the answer. Each city-state put their own **SYMBOLS** on their coins including the owl (Athens), the winged horse, Pegasus (Corinth), an eagle (Olympia), a bee (Ephesus), and on Selinunte's coins, celery!

Coins had an agreed value due to how much gold and silver they contained. Many states did the math and started making their coins slightly lighter than their value. The difference covered the cost of making them. *Sneaky.*

To make the coins, a block of solid metal was carved with one side of the coin's design. A blank coin was placed on the block, then a block with the other side's design was placed on top. The whole lot was hit really **HARD** with a hammer.

Athens dabbled with different coins, but its TETRADRACHM (which would buy you 30–40 kg of wheat) was popular for 400 years. It was the first coin accepted throughout much of the ancient world. Many other coins weren't, which created new job opportunities in moneychanging. Today's exchange rate for tetradrachms is very good… In 2016, one tetradrachm was sold for $613,999!

DON'T BANK ON IT

Arrived in a new place and need your coins swapped for local currency? In ancient Greece, you might head off to the town square or market to find **kollybistés** (moneychangers). A few were reported to be downright dodgy.

It didn't take long before some **MONEYCHANGERS** branched out— lending money and accepting deposits of money or goods.

By 300 BCE or so, most of Greece's banking action had moved out of temples and into homes or onto tables in public spaces. This is where **TRAPEZITAI** (bankers) worked, usually charging 6% interest for loans. Risky loans to traders for ships and trips (from which the loan-taker might not return due to bad weather or attack) had higher interest—often 20–30%.

One **TRAPEZITAI** was Pasiŏn, a slave owned by two Athenians, who worked at the port of Piraeus. Such was Pasiŏn's passion for banking, he made enough money to buy his own freedom. **RESULT!**

As some bankers got wealthy, they bought other businesses. Pasiŏn was no exception, purchasing a shield-making factory and 200 slaves to work in it. With all the wars around, business boomed and he zoomed up Athens' Rich List. He even donated 1,000 shields and an entire trireme—the biggest, baddest warship of the time—to Athens.

I WONDER WHAT IT COULD BE?!

Even with such gifts, Pasiŏn's fortune was said to be worth more than 70 talents—a sum a typical Greek wouldn't earn in 700 years! Other slaves to money in the ancient world weren't so fortunate...

SLAVE TO MONEY

Pasĭon passed on his banking business to another former slave, Phormio. However, most slaves in the ancient world didn't have it that easy. Most slaves in ancient Greece and elsewhere were captured in battles or conquests and bought and sold like you might chickens or cattle. They mostly worked hard, back-breaking jobs in mines, farm fields, and even underwater, diving deep for pearls and sea-sponges.

Some poor people became slaves simply because they couldn't repay loans they had taken out. The creditor (the person owed) might lose their money, but gain a slave, sometimes for life. Families needing money might offer up one of their children as a **DEBT SLAVE** should they fail to repay a loan.

Others who had defaulted on their loans might be forced to work as a slave for no pay for a number of years before they were set free. This is known as **DEBT BONDAGE**, and it has been used as a form of slavery around the world. Although it might be theoretically possible to pay off the debt, food, housing, and clothing for the debtor would add to the total owed, meaning in reality, the debt continually increased.

Athens was one of the first places in the ancient world to outlaw this harsh practice, but it continued elsewhere, including in early Rome where it was called **NEXUM**. Being a Roman nexus was one small step up from being a full-on slave. Sure, you worked for nothing and could still be beaten, but you couldn't be sold on, and it would all be over one day... probably.

Nexum was abolished in 326 BCE, by which time Rome owned its own money-making temple...

FUNDING FIGHTS

The ROMANS are famous for their mighty EMPIRE, spread across most of Europe and North Africa. But before they became **HUGE** in Europe, the Romans found themselves under attack. A tribe of **GAULS** had the gall to invade. Early warning of the sneaky night raid in 390 BCE came from honking geese in the city. As a result, ROME survived.

Feeling grateful, the Romans renamed their goddess of geese (and many other things) **JUNO MONETA** and built a temple dedicated to her in the center of Rome. Moneta is where the word **"money"** comes from. It was also where actual money came from in Rome, because a mint (a place where physical money is made) was set up inside the temple. At first, it produced aes signatum—large bronze bullion (bars) weighing up to 2.5 kg.

Later, the mint made heavy bronze coins called "**ASSES.**" One ass in 300 BCE could buy you a two-night stay in an inn, but a slave needed 10,000 asses to be free.

I WISH I HAD 10,000 ASSES.

I BEG YOUR PARDON?

Around 211 BCE, **DENARII COINS** containing 4.5 g of silver were introduced. Each denarius was worth 10, later 16, asses. They would be Rome's main currency for almost 500 years. Millions were minted. Good job too, since a **BIG** empire came with even **BIGGER** bills.

The ROMAN ARMY might have been key to the empire's success, but it cost an absolute fortune to run. The wages for a single legion of ROMAN SOLDIERS were over 1.5 million denarii (a very large sum)… and that was in peacetime. In war, they cost even more!

WE'RE STILL 3 MILLION DENARII SHORT, EMPEROR!

PERHAPS WE CAN JUST REPLACE ALL THE SOLDIERS WITH GEESE?

ROMAN RISES

Rome had **WALLET WORRIES** besides paying its soldiers. Running a growing empire with a booming population was expensive. Large numbers of Rome's silver and new gold coins (called **AUREUS**) were paid out for imported food and luxuries, as the Romans spent **BIG**!

INDIAN SPICES
3 GOLD COINS
A BAG

I DO FANCY INDIAN TAKEOUT.

Gaining more gold and silver wasn't a problem while the empire expanded and captured more precious metals or land containing mines. But as empire-building slowed, **COIN SHORTAGES** struck Rome.

I THINK THESE COINS ARE WAY TOO LIGHT.

A series of Roman emperors chose to cut the cost of the currency. Coins were either made lighter in weight or less pure by adding other, less valuable metals, including copper, tin, and lead. This is called **DEBASING**.

EMPEROR NERO fiddled with finances in 64 CE. He slashed the amount of silver in denarii coins down to 3.2 g. Losing a little under a gram may not sound a big deal, but the coins lost over a fifth of their value.

Merchants and traders weren't easily fooled. They put their prices up, so they gained more coins to equal the same amount of silver as before. When prices went up, workers demanded more money as wages. This needed yet more coins, which meant rulers were tempted to debase the coins further.

When currency loses value and prices go up, it's called **INFLATION**. The cycle can go on and on. By the 300s, Rome's "silver" coins contained next to no silver. Not long after, the empire began breaking up. Things were about to get *dark and deadly* in Europe.

FINE TIME

The *"Dark"* or *Early Middle Ages* began after Rome fell to invaders in 476 CE and lasted for about 500 years. During this time, parts of northern Europe were ruled by tribal groups such as the Saxons, Franks, Alemanni, and Goths.

I PROPOSE WE CALL THIS NEW ERA...

... THE DARK AGES.

OF COURSE YOU DO.

While money marched on elsewhere, it took a bit of a breather in Britain. No new coins were minted there for around 200 years. Britons went old school—back to bartering—to exchange both their goods and skills.

WE'LL PLAY YOU OUR NEW ROCK OPERA IN EXCHANGE FOR THOSE TURNIPS.

I'LL GIVE YOU MY TURNIPS IN EXCHANGE FOR YOU NOT PLAYING, THANKS.

Over in northern Europe, silver denarii coins were used long after the Romans had gone. Some changed hands as fines for taking another person's life. This became known as **WEREGELD** or **WERGILD** and saw the money paid to the dead person's family or clan.

Different tribes set different rates, but all priced people's lives according to their status. Killing a freeman could cost you 200 silver coins while a priest or cleric might set you back twice as much. If you foolishly murdered a nobleman, the price could be a sky-high 1,200 coins, but killing a slave cost nothing!

The Alemanni charged double for the death of a woman, while the sexist Saxons valued a woman's life at half a man's.

Speaking of Saxons, weregeld spread with them into Britain where the Anglo-Saxon king, Alfred the Great, took it further. In his Dooms (code of laws), he listed weregeld prices for injuries to different parts of the body.

Eye – 66 shillings
Wound below knee – 12 shillings
Chopped off thumb – 20 shillings
Chopped off arm (above elbow) – 80 shillings
Big toe – 20 shillings
Broken leg – 30 shillings
Little toe – 5 shillings
Little finger – 9 shillings
Front tooth – 8 shillings

CHINA'S CHANGING CURRENCIES

By the time weregeld was occurring in northern Europe, many parts of China were already on their third, fourth, or fifth different form of money! Ancient China was made up of lots of separate kingdoms. Some, like the Sung and Wei, used **SALT** as money, while one ruler of the Tchou kingdom issued small sheets of silk. Many kingdoms used cowry shells.

Around 3,000 years ago, some Chinese states stopped shelling out and started cashing in with copper and bronze. These metals were fashioned into the shape of knives (called dao) or spades. Some kingdoms first used knives then switched to spades, while the Chu kingdom used coins stamped with designs resembling ants or ghostly faces.

After centuries of bickering and outright war, the different states of China were united by its first emperor, Qin Shi Huang.

Qin banned a lot of things, including most books and all other currencies. Their replacement were **BAN LIANG** coins, which were round with a square hole in the middle.

Each coin wasn't worth much, but the square hole allowed them to be strung together. In fact, you could get a pretty good if dull job as a qiánpù stringing batches of 100 coins together to form a single 1,000-coin chuàn.

Well, we say a thousand, but it was more like 980, as the qiánpù would take a few coins from the string as payment for their efforts. A completed chuàn could weigh almost 5 kg and was usually carried slung over the shoulder.

Ban liang were replaced by later Chinese emperors, but the square hole and stringing coins together remained. Their sheer weight cried out for something lighter... **FLYING MONEY**!

FLYING CASH

Lugging heavy coin strings around was a real pain. So, the ingenious Chinese turned to another of their inventions—**PAPER**—to create a new type of money.

POSSIBLE ALTERNATIVES TO METAL COINS:

~~FIREWORKS~~

PAPER?

It started during the Tang dynasty (618–907 CE), when Chinese merchants could deposit their coins in a treasury. They received a certificate or receipt, which was much easier to carry or hide and could be turned back into coins when they got back home. The receipt was known as feiqian or "flying cash."

FEIQIAN was nearly—but not quite—actual money: it couldn't buy goods directly. The jiaozi notes issued by the Song dynasty (960–1279 CE) were a little closer. These **BANKNOTES** could be transferred to others or exchanged for coins at government banks. However, they weren't great for savers—some jiaozi notes expired after three years, becoming worthless.

The Yuan dynasty (1271–1368) issued **JIAOCHAO**, paper money that could be used like any coin. The Ming dynasty (1368–1644) went one step further, creating notes that were, er, notable because they were meant to replace coins. Both these notes were only worth the value printed on them because the government said so. The term for this is "**FIAT MONEY**" and it's much like the €, $, £, and many other currencies today.

The Ming made one **BIG** mistake; they kept on printing new notes without recalling the old ones. This led to an awful lot of **INFLATION**, which decreased the notes' value. By 1535, a one-guán note, originally equal to 1,000 copper coins, was worth just ¼ of a coin. Yikes!

While the Ming got into a pickle with paper, everyone else continued with coins.

STONE-COLD RICH

Well, almost everyone. Some of China's neighbors, such as Mongolia, had their money down to a tee... sorry, tea. Bricks of compressed tea leaves—the dosh you could drink— were common currency from the 900s onward.

Meanwhile, east across the Pacific Ocean, the small island of Yap became home to the **BIGGEST , HEAVIEST** money the world had ever seen.

Starting around 1000 CE, circular slabs of **LIMESTONE ROCK** called Rai were quarried from another island, Palau (Yap had no limestone), and floated back on rafts. The 250-km sea journey could be perilous, but the rewards could be great. The bigger and older the stone, the more valuable it was.

HE'S GOT SOME EXPENSIVE WHEELS.

Many Rai were the size of your hand but some were **FAR LARGER.** The biggest stood 12 ft tall and weighed 8,800 lbs—more than a rhino!

These whoppers weren't used to do your food shopping, but for big money transactions such as weddings and to pay ransoms. They changed hands, but rarely changed places—it was too much bother to move the big ones! Everyone just agreed that the stone had a new owner.

Despite being a tiny island with a small population, the people of Yap appeared money-mad. Apart from Rai, they had four other currencies—strings of small shells, big shells, balls of spicy turmeric, and **MMBUL**—material used to make loincloths (which was all a Yap man wore).

WORLD'S WEALTHIEST

The island of **YAP** wasn't the only place with unusual money. Over in Africa, heavy metal crosses (called Katanga) and even potato-mashers acted as cash.

Unlike your kitchen's spud botherer, these mashers were solid iron and called **ENSUBA**. To the Bafia people (who lived in what is now Cameroon), they were both a tool and a currency. With them, you could buy livestock and, er, wives at a price of 30 mashers or so. Scandalous.

The world's wealthiest man didn't make his money in mash. **SALT** and **GOLD** were ancient Africa's two most valuable commodities and **MANSA MUSA** controlled them both when he became leader of the mighty Mali Empire, around 1312 CE. He became extremely rich in the process.

It's hard to put an exact figure, but Musa owned up to half the entire world's known gold—Ker-Ching! Estimates of **$400 billion** make him richer than any person today.

Traveling light wasn't an option for Mr. Moneybags. When making a pilgrimage to Mecca in the 1320s, Musa didn't just throw some things into an overnight bag. No, he traveled with 8,000 courtiers, 12,000 slaves carrying gold bars, and 100 camels each loaded down with 50–120 kg more gold.

Musa's journey was the world's biggest **GOLD GIVEAWAY**. Thousands of kilograms of the precious metal were thrown out to cheering crowds. So much was donated in Egypt that it caused the value of gold there to collapse and not regain its value for over 10 years.

So how to count all these mountains of gold? Well, it depends what number system you use…

WHAT A ROTTA!

TRADING was making some kings and kingdoms very rich. But the different counting systems countries used could slow things down. Most of medieval Europe used Roman numerals, with letters to represent numbers, like II = 2, VIII = 8, and XXI = 21.

Without zero or placeholders (places in bigger numbers for ones, tens, hundreds, and so on), Roman numerals s l o w e d sums down. Fortunately, there was an alternative used by Arab traders. The Arabic-Hindu number system ranged from 0 to 9 and is what we use today.

A young Italian trader from Pisa, called **FIBONACCI**, traveled with his dad to Algeria and then to other places around the Med. He was amazed at the speedy sums Arabic merchants managed using their number system. So, he tried to make it popular back at home, publishing a book, *Liber Abaci*, in 1202. The general public stuck with VIII and XI, but merchants and bankers switched to the new numbers.

Pisa was one of many city-states that made up Italy. They were major centers of trade and banking in Europe. Most banks were similar to those in ancient Greece, one or two people behind wooden benches or tables in squares and plazas. These tables were known as **BANCA**.

A failed banker who lost their money would have their table smashed, and were known as a **BANCA ROTTA** (a broken bank). This is where we get the word "bankrupt" from.

When an individual or a small business goes bankrupt, there's probably not a lot they can do. But when a whole Italian city-state ran out of money, it didn't break benches and tables. It forced all of its people to loan it yet more money…

FAMILIES AND FLORINS

In the early 1170s, Venice was fighting a costly war against the Byzantine Empire. The city issued a **PRESTITI**—a sort of government loan with a difference. People were forced to lend the city their hard-earned money and were promised a small percentage back as a regular payment plus the sum they'd lent… later on. The entire loan financed a fancy fleet of 120 warships, which sailed off to battle…

…and lost… badly. The leader of the fleet and city, Doge Vitale Michiel, was murdered by an angry mob on his return to Venice.

Despite this debt proving deadly, Venice issued more prestiti in the centuries that followed to finance building, expeditions, and wars. When they struggled to repay, the city even held lotteries, with a handful of "winners" merely getting their money back. Whoopee-do!

In 1252, Venice's rival, Florence, minted its first **FLORIN**. This coin contained 0.1 oz of pure gold, and was used widely for almost 300 years. During that time, Italy became the leading center for trade in Europe, and Florence became THE place to make and move money. The city had more than 80 banks—some no longer on tables, but housed inside grand buildings instead.

One Florentine family, the **MEDICI**, became the bankers for much of Europe's royalty. They became worth hundreds of thousands of florins (when you only needed 200 to buy a city house). Two Medici became French queens, while four others became Pope. The family were feared for their ruthlessness, and were rumored to use poisonous plants on rivals, enemies, and even uppity members of their own family.

TAKING STOCK

Remember those prestiti Venice issued? By the 1300s, they could be sold on for less than their full amount if you needed quick money. Some buyers even spread rumors about Venice being in trouble just to worry people and lower the price further. Cheeky!

Other debts and loans in Europe also began to be bought and sold. In 1531, Antwerp in Belgium built an exchange for these trades to take place, and the following century the first STOCK EXCHANGES opened up to buy and sell something called STOCKS AND SHARES.

A company can divide who owns it (its stock) into lots of small fractions, each known as a share. Companies sell some of these shares off to investors to raise money for their business. Investors don't have to do any work for the business, they just sit back and wait…

If the company does well, the value of a share is likely to rise, meaning the investor could sell it for more than they paid for it. But if the company struggles, the price of a share could fall sharply—or even become worthless!

Despite the risk, investors snapped up shares, hoping to make money by selling them on to others later for a much higher price.

More and more companies formed and sold their stock to raise cash. These included Puckle's Machine Company in 1720, which raised money to make guns firing SQUARE cannonballs! No, they didn't do well, and those who paid £8 a share (a LOT at the time) lost out.

Many of the other early companies to sell their stock were set up for trading with Asia or the hotly-contested continents of North and South America. Not long after the explorers, the money men started moving in…

COCOA, COTTON, AND COPPER

A number of amazing civilizations were doing very well in the Americas, thank you, before Europeans arrived with their guns and greed for gold and silver. The AZTECS (of present-day Mexico) had plenty of these metals, but used three quite different things as currency.

The most common was COCOA BEANS—yes, the key ingredient of chocolate. Considered a gift from the gods, set numbers of beans were used to buy other goods—10 would buy you a rabbit, while up to 300 were needed for a length of cotton cloth called quachtli. This cloth was also used as a currency.

You probably don't think of models of garden tools as being valuable, but the AZTECS did. Their highest-value currency, used for trade, were model hoes made of COPPER. Each was worth a whopping 8,000 cocoa beans.

I don't know if you've been grounded or sent to your room for misbehaving. I know I have. However unfair we thought the punishment was, it's nothing compared to being used as currency. Some Aztec parents sold their children into slavery or for human sacrifices! The going rate for a live child was up to 600 cocoa beans.

KIDS THESE DAYS DON'T APPRECIATE THE SACRIFICES WE MAKE FOR THEM.

YOU MEAN OF THEM?

Further to the south, the INCAS had their own mighty empire criss-crossed by thousands of miles of roads. As mentioned earlier (see page 11), the Incas didn't use money, so the gold and silver they found (and they found mountains of it) was fashioned into art or ceremonial items… which attracted the attention of greedy treasure-hunters from Europe.

I'M TELLING YOU… I REALLY HAVE NOTHING OF VALUE.

SUPER SILVER

Tales of vast riches in the Americas inspired bands of European soldiers and treasure-seekers to risk crossing the Atlantic and taking a step into the unknown. **SPANISH CONQUISTADORS** were first in the 1520s and 1530s, overpowering the Aztecs and Incas with guns, steel swords, and horses (an animal the Aztecs and Incas had never seen) and stealing all their riches. Rude!

Now, imagine coming across a mountain, okay, a very large hill, in a foreign land and discovering that it was mostly made of solid silver. It would knock your little conquistador socks off, wouldn't it?

Well, that's precisely what happened when the Spanish reached Potosí (in Bolivia) in the 16th century. They had found the world's richest source of silver—and forced tens of thousands of local people to mine it for them.

At its peak (get it?), Potosí was producing 200,000 kg of silver a year, a **VAST** amount. Much was turned into coins known as "pieces of eight" (because one coin was worth eight **REALES**—Spain's currency at the time). Fleets of ships carrying silver across the Atlantic became targets for pirates.

Despite the pirates' best efforts, silver flooded into Europe and caused prices to rise. But it also boosted trade between Europe (which thirsted after Chinese goods like silks, spices, and porcelain) and China (which didn't care much for European goods, but hankered after silver).

CAN WE INTEREST YOU IN SOME SPAGHETTI?

NO THANKS...

... BUT WE'LL TAKE THE SILVERWARE!

From 1550 to 1800, mines in southern and central America produced over 85% of the world's silver. But north of these regions, other European arrivals in the Americas faced something of a currency **CRISIS**...

PAPER PROBLEM SOLVERS

In 1685, the settlers of New France, a colony in Canada, hadn't received coins from Europe for months. They used **BEAVER PELTS** as money until they ran low.

The governor of New France, **JACQUES DE MEULLES**, had an ace idea. He ordered all the packs of **PLAYING CARDS** in the colony to be sent to him. Then he cut them up, signed and stamped them, and issued them to colonists as cash until the coins arrived.

De Meulles was in de money and had pretty much invented the first fiat currency in North America, just like the Yuan and Ming dynasties did in China (see page 43) and a banker in Sweden did in Europe in 1661.

Sweden had a **COPPER COIN** problem. Its riksdaler coins had become ridiculous. With copper low in value, the currency had grown and grown—becoming copper plates that were 27.5 inches long and weighed up to 40 lbs. At least you wouldn't lose them down a drain or the back of the sofa.

YOUR CHANGE, SIR.

In 1661, Banco Stockholm bigwig Johan Palmstruch began printing credit notes called **KREDITIVSEDLAR** to be used instead of copper. These promised to pay the owner with metal money at a later date and were Europe's first banknotes. Yay!

This portable paper money proved super-popular. So much so, that Johan got greedy and printed far more notes than his bank had metal money as back-up.

Within three years, Palmstruch came unstuck. His bank couldn't repay, failed, and the government stepped in. Johan was sentenced to *DEATH*. In the end, he wasn't executed, but other money men and women would be, just a few years later...

COIN CLIPPERS

Before banknotes, the most common crime concerning money was **CLIPPING**. Clipping is the cutting or shaving off of a little of the metal from a coin, usually its edges, using shears and files.

Usually only a little was taken off each coin, not enough for most people to notice. But all those shavings of silver could quickly mount up into precious metal moolah. The clippers would melt down all the metal fragments to make blocks called **BULLION**, which they would sell to unscrupulous metal dealers—the type who didn't ask too many questions.

Gold and especially silver coin clipping had occurred for centuries. In 1278, more than 600 alleged coin clippers were rounded up and imprisoned in the Tower of London. Around half lost their heads… literally.

The killing of clippers continued for another 500 years*. When Thomas and Anne Rogers' house in Acton, England, was searched in 1690, all sorts of clipping kit and 40 clipped silver coins were found. *Guilty!* The pair met grisly ends. Anne was burnt alive, while Thomas was hung, drawn, and quartered.

Despite the harsh punishments, clipping remained common. So much so, that shopkeepers often used scales to check customers' coins weren't underweight.

HEY, HAVE YOU LOST WEIGHT?

NO, JUST HAD A TRIM.

It took a **BIG** brain to come up with an ingenious solution. That brain belonged to SIR ISAAC NEWTON, scientist, legend, and from 1696, warden of Britain's Royal Mint.

He introduced coins with lots of fine grooves around their edges—known as milling. Shaving or clipping milled coins was instantly noticeable—stopping clippers in their tracks.

*In 1789, coin-clipping Catherine Murphy became the last woman to be burned at the stake in Britain.

NATIONAL BANKS

BANKS were booming in Europe in the 17th century, so it was no surprise that governments started getting in on the act.

Remember Johan Palmstruch from a few pages back? After his bank failed, Sweden set up the Sveriges Riksbank—the first modern central bank. These are **NATIONAL BANKS** that help control the supply of money in a country and may lend money to the government.

In 1694, England was at war with France (this happened a lot in the past) and needed to raise some hard cash to rebuild its navy. The Bank of England was formed to help.

WE'RE GONNA NEED A BIGGER BANK.

The Bank produced the first long-lasting **BANKNOTES** in Europe. These were handwritten and their smallest denomination (amount) was £50. This was at a time when most people earned under £20 a year!

The first £5 notes appeared in 1793, but clerks still had to handwrite in details and sign each one until fully printed notes arrived in 1853.

By this time, the Bank had moved to London's Threadneedle Street. Today, its **GIANT UNDERGROUND VAULTS** contain 5,000 metric tons of gold bars worth £194 billion. They require a spoken password and keys over a foot long to open.

Let's jump back to 1695, when, north of the border, the **BANK OF SCOTLAND** had just opened. 33 years later, they invented the overdraft. This is when a bank allows someone to spend more money than they have in their account on the promise that the overdrawn amount will be paid back. **OVERDRAFTS** proved a boon for businesses waiting for payments from customers.

CENTRAL BANKS sprang up elsewhere, including the **BANQUE DE FRANCE**, set up in 1800 by Napoleon Bonaparte. Battles between "Boney" and Britain would lead to one family becoming the most powerful bankers in Europe.

CASHING IN

In 1798, **NATHAN MAYER ROTHSCHILD** moved from Frankfurt to England. Although he didn't speak English, he set up business in Manchester selling cloth and loaning money. The cloth sold well, but the **LOANS** did better.

It wasn't long before he moved to **LONDON** and set up a bank—all you needed was **LOADSAMONEY**! Rothschild earned a reputation as a provider of fast finance, so much so that the British government trusted him with a top-secret project.

In the 1810s, Britain was at war (yet again) this time with French general, **NAPOLEON "BONEY" BONAPARTE**. The British wanted to get a stack of cash to their general Wellington, who was booting the French out of Spain and pushing them back to the Pyrenees mountains.

Rothschild organized the **SMUGGLING** of hundreds of metric tons of gold across Europe using ships and horse-riding couriers. The gold was converted into local currency to pay Wellington's troops.

Nathan's brothers, Jacob, Carl, Salomon, and Amschel, all established banks in Europe. They communicated using a **SECRET LANGUAGE** and sometimes sent letters via **CARRIER PIGEONS**. When Wellington defeated Napoleon at Waterloo in 1815, Rothschild was the first in England to know, such was the *speed* of his network of informers.

With a fortune worth 0.62% of England's entire income, Rothschild was the **WEALTHIEST MAN** in the country. He even bailed out the Bank of England in 1826 with a massive loan of gold when 145 private banks collapsed. The Rothschilds became the biggest bankers in Europe and Nathan's son would run **BRITAIN'S ROYAL MINT.**

MINTED!

Mints were moving on by the time the Rothschilds were cashing in. Coins, which had been made by hand and simple tools for centuries, started being produced at a great rate by powerful machines.

I'M NOT MAKING MONEY ANY MORE!

PSSSSHHHH! That's the sound of **STEAM** arriving to power factories and industry. James Watt was a big deal in steam engines and his business partner, Matthew Boulton, built the Soho Mint in Birmingham in 1788. It used steam engines to power presses that each stamped out 70–80 coins a minute from sheets of metal.

The Soho Mint struck millions of copper one-penny coins for Britain. The Royal Mint ended up buying Boulton's machines to do it themselves. Boulton also sold machines to Russia and Denmark, and provided millions of blank coins (called **PLANCHETS**) to other countries to create their own designs.

WE NEED TO CHOOSE BETWEEN OUR TWO DESIGNS FOR THESE PLANCHETS...

... IF ONLY WE COULD FLIP SOMETHING FOR IT.

For example, 20 million blanks reached Philadelphia, home of the shiny, new **US MINT**, founded in 1792.

The United States had produced its first national coin five years earlier. The one-cent penny, designed by famous statesman Ben Franklin, had a sun and sundial, the Latin word Fugio (meaning **"I FLEE"**) and **"MIND YOUR BUSINESS,"** all crammed onto one side's design.

Visitors to Philadelphia have flung so many pennies at Franklin's grave they broke the gravestone. It cost 8 million pennies ($80,000) to repair it!

Modern US pennies weigh just 0.09 oz (¼ of a Fugio penny) but they're still far from the lightest coin. That honor goes to the 4–6 mm-wide quarter silver **TARA COIN**, minted in Vijayanagar, India. It weighed a mere 0.002 oz.

Unlike the handmade teensy tara, modern pennies are produced using advanced, computer-controlled machines.

AN UPSETTING BUSINESS

Billions of new coins are minted each year. **MINTING** is no longer as simple as whacking a blank disc of metal with a hammer and hoping. It's a complex process involving computers and even, at the Australian Mint, two robots, Robbie and Titan.

GIANT rolls of **METAL ALLOY** sheet weighing as much as two hippos (3,000 kg) enter a blanking press. These cut out rows of perfect discs—like an **extreme** **COOKIE CUTTER**—at a rate of 6,000 or more coins a minute. The leftover metal, called webbing, is recycled to make new metal rolls.

1.

2.

The blanks are **BAKED** up to 1,740 °F, given a **BATH** in sulphuric acid, and **PUMMELED CLEAN** with **BALL BEARINGS**. A machine called a riddler tests them out. Only perfect blanks get through.

Next step is the **UPSETTING MILL** which creates a raised rim around each blank's edge. The blank has now become a **PLANCHET**. Ta-dah!

Planchets are fed into a stamping machine, which exerts **TONNES OF PRESSURE** on the discs as both sides are stamped with the coin design. This is called "striking." Samples of the struck coins are inspected by microscope.

3.

Any that don't make the grade head for a meeting with the dreaded *waffler* where they are crushed between two high-pressure rollers that create a ridged pattern. This makes them useless, so they're not stolen before recycling.

4.

If all these stages (and more) run smoothly, a mint can churn out coins. The US Mint in Philadelphia produces over **35 MILLION COINS A DAY**— that's mucho money!

5.

THE GREENBACK

Speaking of US money, the **ONE-DOLLAR BILL** ($1) is the most recognizable banknote in the world. There are over 12.4 billion of these notes in circulation—more than one for every person on the planet.

At the height of the **US CIVIL WAR** (1861–65), President Abraham Lincoln ordered production of new money to pay for the war effort. A green ink on the rear gave the dollar its nickname, the greenback. On the front, US Treasury boss Salmon P. Chase stared out sternly. He was replaced in 1869 by the first President, **GEORGE WASHINGTON.**

What a smile! George's dentures were made from hippopotamus ivory.

Early one-dollar bills were pretty large (7.4 x 3.1 inches) and nicknamed **"HORSE BLANKETS."** A bit of an exaggeration, but they were longer than this book is tall.

HOW MANY HORSE BLANKETS DID YOU SPEND ON THIS HORSE BLANKET?

They shrank in 1929 and remain the same size today, with the design barely altered since 1963.

Gorgeous George

Serial number allows banknote to be tracked

All-seeing "eye of providence"

Great Seal of the United States

13 pyramid steps

13 arrows

Unfinished Egyptian-styled pyramid

13 olive leaves

We call dollar bills "paper" money, but they're actually three-quarters **COTTON** and one-quarter **LINEN**, with blue and red threads woven through. Each note costs 7.7 cents to produce and typically lasts less than six years before it's taken out of circulation.

Old banknotes cannot be recycled due to the ink and threads they contain, so they are shredded. Most are burnt or sent to landfills, although souvenir packs of shredded dollars have been sold.

In 1914, one dollar would buy you four or five German marks. Nine years later, it would net you a billion times more.

MARK MY WORDS

Remember inflation from page 37? Well, **HYPERINFLATION** is inflation that runs wild. It occurs when a currency collapses, people don't trust it, and governments print and flood the economy with vast amounts of new money. This causes prices to soar as the currency's worth plummets.

ARRGGH, IT'S HYPERINFLATION!

In the early 1920s, Germany was suffering from the effects of losing World War I and forking out mega-money as **WAR REPARATIONS** (payments to other nations). The government printed more and more marks (Germany's currency) but **INFLATION GREW** and **GREW**. It reached 29,500% in October 1923, meaning prices doubled every 3.7 days.

People's wage rises could not keep up with price rises. How could they? A loaf of bread that cost 250 marks in January 1923, cost 200,000 million 11 months later. Ouch!

Savings and even newly printed banknotes became worthless and were used as wallpaper or given to children to play with. Many Germans switched to bartering treasured possessions for basic food.

A similar event after World War II left **HUNGARIANS** hungry and their savings in tatters. At its peak in 1946, prices doubled every 15 hours. Yikes!

Hungary's currency, the pengő, became next-to-worthless. So, **BIGGER** and **BIGGER** denomination notes were printed. The largest that reached the public was a 100 million billion pengő banknote—that's 100,000,000,000,000,000,000! It was worth just 20 US cents or less than 10 pence!

In both Hungary's and Germany's cases, changes in government and new currencies helped tackle **HYPERINFLATION**, but which other European nation in the 1920s had its own money misery?

MAKING MONEY

The answer is **PORTUGAL**, the victim of a **MASSIVE** banknote crime.

Its mastermind was **ARTUR ALVES REIS**, a Portuguese conman who just couldn't stop forging. First, he created a fake Oxford University degree to get a job as an engineer. Then, he forged cheques to buy railway and car businesses.

YOU'VE GOT THE WRONG GUY...

I'VE NEVER FORGED ANYTHING IN MY LIFE!

WANTED

While spending 54 days in jail for a previous crime, he hatched an outrageous plan to trick the official printers of Portugal's money (the **ESCUDO**) into printing 100 million, all for him. He forged documents stating that the **500-ESCUDO NOTES**, 200,000 of them, were for the Portuguese colony of Angola. The sum equaled 1% of Portugal's **ENTIRE** economy.

The money entered Portugal in 1925 and he started exchanging the notes for US dollars and UK pounds. Soon, there were as many fake 500-escudo notes in circulation as there were genuine ones.

ALVES REIS hadn't finished. Next, he tried to buy enough shares with his newfound wealth to own **PORTUGAL'S NATIONAL BANK**. What better way of covering up his crimes than being in charge of the very organization he'd cheated? It was a very sneaky ploy... but unfortunately for Alves, not quite sneaky enough. By the end of 1925, suspicions had grown and he was arrested.

People's confidence in their currency fell and the government was overthrown by the army the following year. Alves Reis was sentenced to 20 years in prison—but he wasn't the only one in money trouble, as by the end of the 1920s, cash was about to crash worldwide.

CRASH!

The 1920s saw the arrival of many **EXCITING NEW GOODS**—from radios to fridges to cars. These all cost large sums, so people, particularly in America, bought them on **INSTALLMENT PLANS**. These were like loans, with people repaying an amount every month.

THE WALL STREET CRASH

Business seemed to be **BOOMING**, but lots of companies and people over-borrowed, overspent, and got into *serious debt*. Many also risked their money, investing in shares. In October 1929, things went terribly wrong.

America's stock market **CRASHED**. In New York City, Wall Street, where many US financial businesses were (and are) based, went into panic mode as more and more investors sold their shares. The share prices fell and fell.

By July 1932, the stock market was worth just 11% of what it was in September 1929. Terrible!

Banks and businesses closed, many farms failed, and by 1933, a third of all US workers had no jobs. Unable to repay their debts, many lost their homes. America was in the *Great Depression*, which lasted through much of the 1930s.

I FAIL TO SEE WHAT'S SO GREAT ABOUT ALL THIS.

Other countries suffered, especially those in Europe that traded a lot with America or had been loaned money by US banks. Millions more worldwide lost their jobs and felt money misery.

When economies slump and fewer things are bought and sold than before, we call it a **RECESSION**. The Great Depression was a particularly **BIG** one, but there have been others since. Economists (people who study money and economies) use various measures to judge if a country is in recession. One of these is called GDP.

WEALTH OF NATIONS

The *Great Depression* saw many nations strapped for cash. But how do you measure how much money a country actually has? One way is **GDP** (gross domestic product).

Thought up by US economist Simon Kuznets in the 1930s, it's the **TOTAL VALUE** of all **GOODS** (such as a banana or video game) and **SERVICES** (such as a haircut) produced in a country.

GDP isn't perfect. It doesn't include the parts used to make an item for sale. Nor does it include the valuable work performed by volunteers, by unpaid carers, or the underground economy—people earning money in shady ways...

The US, China, Japan, and Germany (in that order) have the world's **BIGGEST** GDPs. Tiny Pacific islands like Tuvalu and Nauru have the SMALLEST.

By comparing the **GDP** every three months (moneyheads call this "per quarter"), you can see whether a country's economy is growing or shrinking. This is called the GDP growth rate. Now, obviously, a country with 300,000 people is likely to have a smaller GDP than one with 300 million. So, economists sometimes use **GDP PER CAPITA**.

$$\text{This is simply} \quad \frac{\text{GDP}}{\text{Population}}$$

At the start of 2020, top and bottom of the GDP per capita charts were (in US dollars):

TOP

Qatar 138,910
Luxembourg 112,045
Singapore 105,689
Ireland 86,988
Brunei 85,011

BOTTOM

Niger 1,152
Eritrea 1,103
DR Congo 873
Central African Republic 864
Burundi 724

If you're interested, the US figure was $62,606 (10th on the list).

OPPORTUNITY KNOX

One place in the United States holds more gold than the entire GDP of 100 different nations. Found in Kentucky, it's the United States Bullion Depository, AKA **FORT KNOX**.

The US, like many nations, keeps hold of lots of gold as a **RESERVE**. This is a big store of value that can be used to support the country's currency if there's a crisis.

I'VE GOT A SERIOUS CRISIS...

... THE ICE CREAM MAN'S HERE AND I DON'T HAVE ANY CHANGE!

In spring 2020, **FORT KNOX** held 4,583 metric tons of gold, in **IDENTICAL GOLD BARS**, worth a cool $237 billion. That's more than the entire GDP of Portugal, Greece, or New Zealand.

Back in the mid-1930s, much of the US's gold reserves were stored in New York and Philadelphia—two cities on the coast. Fearful that Germany or another enemy might invade and steal, the gold was moved to its new safe place in two trips, in 1937 and 1941. So, how safe is **FORT KNOX**?

For starters, it's next to a **BIG ARMY BASE** holding over 20,000 soldiers and is surrounded by security cameras, electric fences, and minefields. It's also guarded by special **US MINT POLICE**. The **20-METRIC TON VAULT DOOR** is bomb proof and made of 21-inch-thick steel.

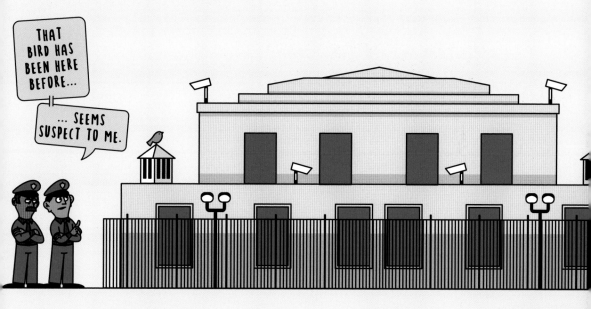

No one person knows how to open the vault. Instead, certain people each have part of the combination, that they and only they know.

It has also held priceless documents, a huge quantity of medicine in case of World War III, and the crown jewels of Hungary.

But you don't need a giant underground vault to keep all your money in one place. These days, all it takes is a little plastic card.

81

PUT IT ON PLASTIC

In 1946, banker John Biggins paid for his meal not with cash but using his brand new **CHARG-IT CARD**. Biggins's bank paid the restaurant later, giving him a convenient, **CASHLESS** way to pay.

Charg-It was a local experiment, but **CREDIT CARDS** became a hit nationwide in the 1950s. All were pieces of cardboard until American Express debuted a **PLASTIC CARD** in 1959. In the 1970s, information began being held on a card's magnetic strip. In many modern cards, microchips perform that task.

Credit cards offer what's called revolving credit. When you spend using a card, you're actually **BORROWING MONEY**. You can borrow up to a set amount (your credit limit). As you pay back what you've borrowed or spend again, the amount of available credit you have keeps on changing. The card companies make money by charging you interest on what you still owe them.

Until 1974, American women couldn't get their own card unless a man was named as an account-holder. Outrageous! Today, there are thought to be over a billion credit cards in the US alone. All **STACKED UP**, they'd tower 86 times taller than Mount Everest.

CREDIT CARDS can be convenient and useful in emergencies. But they have also been accused of making people feel richer than they are, spending more on plastic than they earn, and falling into deep debt. In 2017, total credit card debt in the US reached a massive **ONE TRILLION DOLLARS**.

A different kind of plastic began playing its part in banknotes in the 1980s, due to some Australian antics...

PLAYING WITH PLASTIC

In 1966, **AUSTRALIA** changed currencies from pound to dollar. Before Aussies got used to their new banknotes, five forgers decided to strike.

Mutton, Code, Adam, Papworth, and Kidd **FORGED** 80,000 new $10 notes in secret. That was a lot of money: at the time, workers earned about $60 a week. Some of the notes were buried in Mutton's back garden, but others stayed in circulation long after the gang was caught.

Australians were now distrustful of their new $10 notes. Some even refused to be paid with them. The governor of Australia's Reserve Bank, Nugget Coombs, asked scientists for a different design.

It took a while, but in 1988 Australia debuted their new **POLYMER BANKNOTES**. More than 25 other countries have since followed Australia's lead including Canada, Mexico, and in 2016, the UK. Made from thin **FLEXIBLE PLASTIC**, the new notes were **WATERPROOF** and didn't **TEAR** or **CRUMPLE** easily.

Polymer notes cost more to make, but tend to last 2–3 times longer and are much harder to forge. This is partly due to new security features, including clear plastic windows and 3D images.

On Australia's latest $10 bill, tilting the note causes a **COCKATOO'S WINGS** to flap up and down and the number 10 to change direction. Shining a light through a see-through **MAPLE LEAF** on Canada's new polymer notes projects the number of dollars the note is worth.

Most people's first experience of these new notes is when they pop out of another newish development—a "hole in the wall" machine.

HOLES IN THE WALL

The year 1967 was a **groovy** time for music and money. It saw the arrival of machines that let people get their hands on their cash outside normal bank opening hours. The first, invented by **JOHN SHEPHERD-BARRON**, paid out just one £10 note per go in London.

These **AUTOMATED TELLER MACHINES** (ATMs) are also known as **CASH POINTS**, dispensers, or holes-in-the-wall. Some early machines kept your bank card after each use—it had to be posted back to you afterward! Today, after being read inside the machine, the card pops out seconds before your cash—a deliberate design feature to help stop you forgetting it.

There are nearly 4 million **ATMs** around the world, including floating ones on ferries and two at McMurdo Station in chilly Antarctica. There are mobile ATMs built into buses in India and one fitted inside a giant elephant sculpture at Dusit Zoo, Thailand.

For security, most machines require a four-digit **PERSONAL IDENTIFICATION NUMBER** (PIN). ATMs in Japan and Brazil scan a person's hand or finger print to check their identity.

ATM

THIS MACHINE IS GREAT - IT NEVER FORGETS TO GIVE MY CARD BACK!

Sadly, thousands of *cash machine crimes* occur every year. Some involve criminals fitting tiny cameras into ATMs, which film the card number and a user entering their PIN. The criminal can then clone (copy) the card and use it.

WE'RE ONLY TRYING TO STEAL THEIR DETAILS, NOT WIN AN OSCAR!

ATM

CUT!

Others try to break into machines. Some get a nasty surprise. **DYE PACKS,** triggered by the door being forced, may spray the banknotes and the thief with permanent red or purple dye, making the notes useless and the robber easy to detect.

WAS IT ANY OF THESE, MISS?

ATMs may offer cash convenience, but many people have no access to banks or cash at all.

MICROBANKS

We might think of banks as a normal part of every main street, but millions of people, particularly in poorer nations, have **NO ACCESS TO BANKS**. They may lack bank accounts and the money to put in them.

They may also lack **ASSETS**—valuable items (such as a house) they can offer a bank as security when getting a loan. These assets can be used as something called collateral, which means they can be taken by the bank if the borrower fails to repay a loan.

Many poor people only want to borrow tiny sums of money, too small to interest regular banks. When economics professor **MUHAMMAD YUNUS** hiked to a rural Bangladeshi village in 1975, he was shocked to find a group of women wanting a loan of just $27. They made bamboo chairs, but couldn't afford to buy bamboo at a fair price without the loan. He offered the money himself at zero interest.

I'LL LOAN YOU SOME MONEY IF YOU'LL LOAN ME A CHAIR!

Yunus later set up the **GRAMEEN BANK**—a **MICROBANK** to provide similar small loans.

NEXT CUSTOMER...

... WELCOME TO THE MICROBANK!

Many more microbanks followed. They lend small sums to enable people to start or continue small, local businesses. Some have been criticized for letting extremely poor people get into debt. But, in many cases, **MICROLOANS** have enabled people to run a small business and climb out of extreme poverty.

By the time Yunus and the Grameen Bank won the **NOBEL PEACE PRIZE** in 2006, the bank had made over 9 million microloans to people, 97% of them to women. The average amount borrowed was $100.

Microbanks have since been joined by other ways of bypassing regular banks to raise funds or gain loans.

I USED MY MICROLOAN TO SET UP MY SMALL BUSINESS.

BEYOND BANKS

Instead of asking a single bank or person for one big loan, **CROWDFUNDING** sees people ask for small donations from lots of members of the public. Projects are publicized via the internet and social media. Rock band Marillion were the first online crowdfunders, raising $60,000 for a US tour in 1997.

Today, millions of pleas for funds are found online, mostly via crowdfunding websites like **INDIEGOGO** and **GOFUNDME**. People hope to raise enough online pledges to reach their target. In many cases, if they do not, the money is returned to donors.

One of the biggest crowdfunding success stories was **OCULUS**. In 2012, they raised $2.5 million for their Rift virtual-reality headset. Two years later, the company was sold to Facebook for a cool $2 billion!

KICKSTARTER is the biggest crowdfunding site. Starting in 2009, it has seen more than $4.8 billion pledged to projects with over 180,000 successfully funded. These range from new movies and inventions to weird stuff like toilet bowl nightlights, crystal bacon earrings, and—I kid you not—anti-zombie soap.

People can also lend their own money to others directly, without using banks. **PEER-TO-PEER** (P2P) lending began in the 2000s and acts a little like a dating agency, matching wannabe borrowers to one or more potential lenders online.

Lenders get to choose who their money goes to and often get a higher rate of interest than they would with a bank. P2P, though, has big risks. People might not always get their loaned-out money back.

Sharing money with peers is one thing. But what about sharing your whole currency? Some countries have done just that.

EURO MOST WELCOME

A **CURRENCY UNION** is when two or more countries all choose to use the same money. Eight island states in the Caribbean all use the Eastern Caribbean Dollar, for instance.

The largest ever currency union was created in 2002. It involved 12 members of the **EUROPEAN UNION**: Austria, Belgium, Finland, France, Germany, Greece, Ireland, Italy, Luxembourg, the Netherlands, Portugal, and Spain. They all agreed to bid farewell to their old currencies and adopt the same new one, the **EURO** (€).

The idea was to strengthen ties between the countries and make it easier for business between them without changing currencies all the time. Visitors and business from outside the **EUROZONE** also find it easier to deal with just one currency.

The **BIGGEST** currency changeover ever took a lot of work. A staggering 14.89 billion euro banknotes had to be printed before e-day on January 1st, 2002. Laid end-to-end, they would have s t r e t c h e d to the Moon and back 2½ times easily. Some 53 billion coins had to be minted, then moved around. In the Netherlands alone, distributing the new coins took 8,000 truck trips.

Another seven nations have since joined the **EUROZONE**, giving it a population of over 340 million. The currency they use features the same banknotes, but the coins have one common side and the other stamped with each country's own design—the owl of Athens (see page 28) for Greece's €1 coin for example.

While the fact that Slovenia chose to include a €3 coin is a little odd, that's nothing compared to some of the weird and wonderful wonga from around the world.

MAKING MONEY FROM MONEY

NUMISMATISTS are people who study and collect money for fun, interest, or investment—hoping to sell at a profit in the future. **NATIONAL MINTS** also like to make money by producing commemorative coins to sell to collectors.

> AND HERE, YOU SEE THE LION ON THE OBVERSE SIDE...

ROMAN EMPEROR AUGUSTUS WAS A KEEN COIN COLLECTOR, 2000 YEARS AGO.

Nearly all regular coins in circulation are only worth their **FACE VALUE**. But the mintage of a coin—the total number produced—can make some coins more valuable. Only 20,000 of Monaco's 2007 €2 coins were minted; they're each worth €2000 today! The 2009 UK 50-pence coin celebrating Kew Gardens is now worth 250 times its face value.

> WELL, **ONE** THINKS IT'S A **VERY** VALUABLE FACE!

The 50p has an unusual heptagonal (seven-sided) shape. But it's far from the oddest coin around. How about Bangladesh's flower-shaped 10-poisha, Poland's fan-shaped 10-zloty, or Somalia's one-dollar electric-guitar-shaped coins, minted in 2004?

Then there's those with **UNUSUAL FEATURES** such as the 2007 Cook Islands 10-dollar coin, which features a pop-up moai statue from Easter Island.

MIND IF I BORROW THAT FOR THE VENDING MACHINE?

IT DOESN'T TAKE PRICELESS ARCHAEOLOGICAL ARTEFACTS.

Not to be outdone, another Pacific Ocean island, Palau, produced scratch-n-sniff coins that either smelled of coconut or the ocean. Liberia, in Africa, minted a 10-dollar coin with a piece of real **METEORITE** (space rock) embedded in it.

ODDEST OF ALL? Possibly, the 2007 500-tugrik coin from Mongolia. It plays a sound clip of US President John F. Kennedy saying "Ich bin ein Berliner." So, that's a Mongolian coin featuring an American president speaking German... worth about 18¢. Confused yet?

While these are examples of some of the more "out there" approaches to coinage, most money-making is a little more **RESERVED**.

FEELING RESERVED

People **DEPOSIT** money in banks to earn interest, to use payment methods like debit cards and checks, and for banks' ability to keep their money safe and secure…

… most of the time. When a bank makes a loan, it very rarely hands it over in cash.

Instead, banks type the loan amount into their computer system. As if by *magic*, brand new money is created and credited—added electronically—to the loanee's bank account. Ta-Dah!

This is basically how most of the new money in the world is created. You see, banks only have to hold on to a little of the money that's deposited with them. This is called a **FRACTIONAL BANKING RESERVE** and results in lots more cash swirling around.

FRACTIONAL RESERVE BANKING

WOO HOO!

Jim deposits $1000 in VerySafe Bank. Lucky Jim! Spendable total: **$1000**.

VerySafe Bank's reserve is 10%, so it holds $100 in "reserve" and lends out the remaining $900 to Judy. Spendable total: **$1900**.

Judy buys a new sofa with her $900 loan. Softee Sofas deposits the money in another bank, TopSecure Bank.

This second bank keeps $90 in reserve and loans $810 to Jihan. Spendable total: **$2710**.

Jihan buys $810's worth of apples at the market. The stall holder deposits the $810 in her account held at VerySafe Bank.

HOW MANY APPLES DO YOU WANT?!

VerySafe Bank can then loan out up to $729 (90%) of this sum. Spendable total: **$3439**.

So, from one loan of **$1000**, there's already **$3439** in the system. That's money magic!

Fractional reserve banking works until many bank customers want to withdraw (take out) all of their money at the same time. This is known as **A RUN ON THE BANK** (not a bank on the run) and it can lead to a bank having to borrow lots of money quickly itself or the bank **FAILING**.

THE GLOBAL FINANCIAL CRISIS

In 2008, the world of banking and money experienced an epic **FAIL**. This was a super-complex set of events, but we're gonna try and sum it up in one page. Wish us luck!

Banks like giving loans to borrowers who can pay them back, because the bank earns interest. But if a borrower can't pay them back, the bank **LOSES** the money.

Until the early aughts, house prices in America soared, and banks lent **WILDLY**, including **BIG** money to higher-risk customers (known as subprime loans). The banks assumed these customers could pay back their home loans if they needed to, by selling their houses.

When house prices started falling in 2006, more and more subprime loans weren't repaid to the banks, which then lost over $500 billion—that's more than the entire GDP of Argentina or South Africa. Ouch!

FAMILY, FIVE HOUSES AND SIX CARS TO SUPPORT.

BANKER

When a bank loses too much money, it can no longer pay savers and businesses who use it to keep their money. So when a bank **FAILS**, loads of other people lose their money too, coming down like a house of cards. Most banks invest internationally, so banks and businesses collapsed all around the world. **PANIC!** Whole countries suffered **MASSIVE** debt crises.

Many governments had to spend billions and billions in tax money (known as bail-outs) to keep the banks going. While they were at it, governments had to help out hundreds of other companies. The bills were **EYE-WATERING**.

As a result, the world entered the **GREAT RECESSION**. During this latest not-so-great Great thing (see page 77), millions of people lost savings, jobs, or their homes. Confidence in banks remained low and some people started using cryptocurrencies—money held on computers with no banks involved.

BITCOIN BEGINS

In 2008, an exciting new form of digital money was announced called **BITCOIN**. Invented by the mysterious **SATOSHI NAKAMOTO**, Bitcoin was a form of **CRYPTOCURRENCY**. These are made using encryption (code-making) computing and only exist on computer networks.

Shady Satoshi has never been traced. All these years and still no one knows his, her, or their true identity.

BITCOIN allows money to pass between two people without banks or governments getting involved. It is hard to counterfeit, users can stay private (shhhh), and there's a permanent record of every Bitcoin transaction that has ever happened kept online.

Each time a transaction takes place, a **BLOCK** (a record of the transaction) is added to the complete record called the **BLOCKCHAIN**. All of this gobbles up huge amounts of computing power, so to keep the currency up and running uses vast amounts of electricity—in 2020, the University of Cambridge estimated that Bitcoin uses more electricity each year than the whole of Greece or Switzerland!

CRYPTOCURRENCIES like Bitcoin have no legal value and are only worth what people will pay for them. And that has gone ᵘᵖ and ᵈᵒʷⁿ dramatically. In 2009, one Bitcoin was worth less than 1¢. A Norwegian computer student, Kristoffer Koch, spent $27 to buy 5,000 of 'em for a giggle (actually, a college project) and then forgot all about them...

When he did remember, in 2013, they were worth $850,000. Ker-Ching!

In 2010, Laszlo Hanyecz wanted a slice of the action, so made the first real-world transaction using Bitcoins. He paid ฿10,000 for two large pizzas. By January 2021, the Bitcoins he spent would have been worth over $465 million. Mamma mia!

Speaking of riches, money is not distributed evenly around the world, but just how unevenly may be a surprise...

RICH AND POOR

A handful of people have gotten rich trading in Bitcoin. Many more have made their money in business or inherited wealth from their families. Is being a **MILLIONAIRE** rare and special?

When you read reports about global millionaires, they normally mean those who have wealth over $1 million—the US dollar is king. In 2020, there were 46.8 million such people—about the population of Spain. So not **THAT** rare.

However, those millionaires make up only a tiny 0.6% of all the people on the planet (7.8 billion and counting). But together, they own a massive 44% of all the world's wealth. And there's more!

In 2020, the charity Oxfam reported that the world's 2,153 **BILLIONAIRES** owned more wealth than a total of 4.6 billion other people. Mind-blowing!

JUST ADDING TO MY PIGGY BANK.

THE 43RD WEALTHIEST PERSON ON THE PLANET (WITH $18.6 BILLION) IS A PIG BREEDER, QIN YINGLIN.

Vast **INEQUALITIES** also exist in individual countries. In the US, for example, the richest three men, count 'em, **ONE** (Elon Musk of Tesla and SpaceX), **TWO** (Amazon's Jeff Bezos), **THREE** (Microsoft man Bill Gates), own more than the poorest 160 million Americans put together.

Speaking of the poorest, picture yourself living on less than $1.90 every day for all your food, clothes, medicine, and somewhere to live. Hard to imagine isn't it? Yet, more than 700 million people live in such extreme poverty each year.

And the **WORLD BANK** estimates that the economic impact of the 2020 coronavirus pandemic will see a further 40–60 million fall into the poorest on the planet. The virus has also resulted in more use of electronic money and less of hard, physical cash.

THE END OF HARD CASH?

In 2014, the world's largest personal check was written by a divorced husband, Harold Hamm, to his ex-wife, Sue. The sum? A cool $974,790,317 and 77 cents.

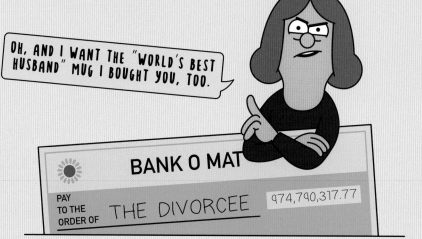

OH, AND I WANT THE "WORLD'S BEST HUSBAND" MUG I BOUGHT YOU, TOO.

BANK O MAT

PAY TO THE ORDER OF THE DIVORCEE 974,790,317.77

Big **CHECKS** and cash may still be around, but a staggering 97% of all the UK's money is not found in banknotes and coins. Not even those big buckets of coins people collect for charity.

It's all stored as bytes of computer memory and accessed via accounts and devices connected to computer networks. **ELECTRONIC CURRENCY** has allowed some pretty nifty innovations—from debit cards to contactless payments using a card or smartphone. In February 2020, there were 723 million contactless payments made in the UK alone.

EARLY ATTEMPTS AT CONTACTLESS PAYMENT

Spending electronically is usually quick and easy, your pocket isn't stuffed full of cash, and it feels safer both for individuals and businesses who aren't left with stacks of money to guard.

There are still plenty of **costs**, though—from providing card-scanning machines to investing in computer security to stop hackers getting into their computers and stealing cash. In 2015, Russian computer hackers were thought to have stolen over $765 million from 100 different banks in the previous 20 months. Ouch!

It may not all be over for cash quite yet, though. Cash remains super-simple, private, and doesn't need internet access, a computer network, or a charged-up smartphone to use it.

Nor does it need a bank account. Here's another surprising fact... As many as 14 million adults in the US don't have a bank account. Worldwide, that figure's close to 1.7 billion. So, cash is likely to stick around well into the future.

FUTURE MONEY

For thousands of years, money has adapted and changed—from barter to Bitcoin. No one knows precisely what will happen in the future, but it's fun to guess!

When it comes to predictions, the smart money's on, er, **SMART MONEY**. Money might become programmable and flow solely as electronic signals between devices. This could lead to some interesting innovations. For example...

As soon as your **SMART TRAINERS** register your 10,000th step of the day, a signal sends a small payment to your electronic account as part of a future health scheme.

Objects might contain **BUILT-IN WALLETS** in their electronics. You may have to pay extra for the object to unlock certain features and if you don't pay off your installments, the object could lock you out altogether.

Your future **SMART VEHICLE** might charge you for each journey based on speed and distance and even subtract money from your account as a fine for every second you go over the speed limit.

Another possibility is that **YOU** become the money, paying by having your body parts scanned to check your identity before money is taken electronically from your account.

Other future possibilities include more shared currencies, like the euro. The nations of Africa are discussing a currency union that could happen in the 2020s, with a single currency called the Afriq or the Afro.

Could the distant future bring a single world currency? What would it be called? How would it be run? Imagine the squabbling over who's in charge.

Alternatively, no one might be in charge as the world currency is stored as a giant blockchain, like Bitcoin, only much, MUCH **BIGGER.**

Whether smart or dumb, digital or physical, one thing's certain. Money is likely to be around for a long time to come.

TIMELINE

~3500 BCE
Banking and loans of goods develop in Mesopotamia around the same time as the first written language—handy to keep records of who owes what to whom.

PRE-5000 BCE
Commodities like cows and cereal crops are used to gift, trade, and swap with others.

1023
China, the first country to master printing, establishes a new government bureau that circulates the world's first permanent, government-issued banknotes.

ALL IT NEEDS NOW IS SOME OLD GUY'S FACE!

1472
Banca Monte dei Paschi di Siena (1472) is set up to grant loans to "the poor or miserable" and is thought of by many as the oldest surviving bank in the world.

1545
The world's largest deposit of silver, a mound almost 6 miles in circumference, is discovered by Spanish conquistadors in Potosí, Bolivia. The Spanish mine and ship thousands of metric tons of silver back to Europe.

~1400 BCE

Cowry shells are used as money in China. They are later followed by imitation shells made of bronze.

~620 BCE

The first standard metal coins with a set weight and value are minted in the kingdom of Lydia (in present day Turkey).

864 CE

The world's oldest surviving mint, the Monnaie de Paris, is officially founded in France by Charlemagne, king of the Franks. It first produced livre, sol, and denier coins.

510 BCE

The tetradrachm silver coin from the Greek city-state of Athens is in wide circulation. It is the first coin that is widely accepted by other states and kingdoms around the Mediterranean.

1602

The first organized stock exchange or stock market is set up in Amsterdam. It is followed by stock markets in Paris (1724), Philadelphia (1790), and London (1801).

1862

The US one-dollar bill enters circulation. Seven years later, the banknote's design is changed to feature the first US president, George Washington. In 1928, the banknotes are shrunk to the size they still are today.

1923

Germany suffers extreme hyperinflation with prices doubling every three or four days. Wheelbarrows of cash won't buy you enough food, not a sausage. It's the wurst!

THE WALL STREET CRASH

1929

The Wall Street Crash occurs when US stocks tumble, ruining the savings of millions of investors. It triggers the Great Depression in which almost half of America's banks close and millions lose their jobs.

1995

The world's first contactless payment card is brought in by the Seoul Bus Transport Association in South Korea. The Upass, as it's now called, was copied by many cities around the world.

1996

After dipping a toe in the water with a 1988 $10 bill, Australia becomes the first country to use polymer (plastic) for all of its banknotes.

1999

Eleven nations, all part of the European Union, agree to replace their own currencies with a single currency, the euro. By the time euro coins and banknotes are in use in 2002, Greece has joined, making it a round dozen of Eurozone members.

2007-08

The global financial crisis starts in the US but spreads throughout the world. Many banks and other financial companies fail while governments spend billions on propping up the financial system.

1959

American Express introduces the first plastic credit card.

1971

Britain goes decimal. It changes its currency from £1 = 240 pence to £1 = 100 pence. Some people haven't stopped grumbling about it since.

1994

The first item sold on the World Wide Web using a credit card is a copy of Sting's album *Ten Summoner's Tales* (for $12.48 + postage). Spotting the potential for mega millions were Pierre Omidyar (devisor of eBay) and Jeff Bezos who began Amazon. Both launched the following year.

2009

Bitcoin, the first major cryptocurrency, is launched.

2020

The global coronavirus crisis causes economies around the world to worsen, as businesses fail due to customers staying safe at home—not shopping, eating at restaurants, or going on vacation.

MONEY AND YOU!

Now, you might only obtain a measly allowance or earn a small amount from odd jobs, but that's no excuse for not managing your money. Looking after your cash is pretty easy. All you need to do is keep track of four figures.

INCOME is the money that flows in, to you and your piggy bank. Yay!

WEALTH is assets you own, such as money in a savings account that pays interest.

EXPENDITURES is simply money you spend. Boo!

DEBT is what you owe to other people. Double boo!

WHERE HAVE YOU BEEN?

Tracking what you spend is hard, but well worth it. Write down every time you splash the cash and review each month. You might be surprised at where your money goes.

Income higher than expenditures? Result! You can tuck some money away as **SAVINGS**. Your parents can help you open a savings account, which pays you extra money as interest. Interested?

Saving can be hard, especially when you have little income, yet there's sooooo much you'd like to buy. There are plenty of ways to help you put a little aside each month.

- Try to walk rather than pay train or bus fares.
- Do odd jobs for neighbors or relatives for a small fee.
- Pack snacks and lunches from home rather than buy from fast-food outlets.
- Don't splash out on bottled water. Fill reusable bottles with tap water instead.
- Spot and use 2-for-1 and money-off deals on movie tickets and other fun things.
- Pop any spare money in a savings box or pay into an account.

Try not to dip into your savings. Leave it, and it will grow and grow. The easiest way to save, of course, is to not buy…

AND THEY SAID THOSE MAGIC BEANS WERE A FRIVOLOUS PURCHASE.

BUY, BYE, BYE

Not buying not only saves you money, it helps save the planet. Our world is already jam-packed with stuff and buy-buy-buy can mean saying hi-hi-hi to lots more packaging, waste, and pollution.

We're not being spoilsports, honest. Just think carefully about whether you really do need to make a purchase.

IS IT SOMETHING I COULD BORROW OR SWAP FOR?

DO WE HAVE SOMETHING LIKE THAT AT HOME?

CAN I REPAIR OR UPGRADE WHAT I HAVE?

CAN I REFILL OR REUSE IT RATHER THAN BUYING A WHOLE NEW ONE?

CAN I DO WITHOUT IT?

I'LL GIVE YOU 400 HEAD OF CATTLE FOR THAT BOARD.

Some of these questions can lead to fun, **MONEY-SAVING SOLUTIONS**—from upgrading your old bike to going back to barter and organizing a swap shop with friends.

Next time you're online or out shopping and something catches your eye...

1. STOP! Ask yourself do you really need the item? I mean, really need it. Give yourself at least a week to think about it. By that time, you'll know if it's still a must-have or just a passing fancy.

2. If you intend on buying something, do your **DETECTIVE WORK**. Search online and in different stores to compare prices (don't forget shipping + handling)—they can vary greatly.

3. Look out for **SALES, SPECIAL OFFER VOUCHERS**, and **DISCOUNT CODES**. Sometimes, more than one discount can be stacked together, meaning bigger savings. BUT don't get lured into buying something for the sake of its slashed, sale price. It's not a bargain if you don't really want it or need it.

4. Is it something that can be bought cheaper **SECONDHAND**, either online or at a local charity shop or thrift store?

If you follow these guidelines, you should find yourself avoiding a lot of unecessary expenditure that you might otherwise regret!

MONEY MISHAPS

A games console and game together cost $220. If the game costs $200 less than the console, what's its price?

Loads of people answer $20. They're **WRONG**—if the total is $220, and the game costs $200 less than the console, then the game is $10 and the console $210. It just shows how quickly one can get into a money muddle.

If you don't pay attention to money matters, they can prove expensive. Ask the people who forget to check the card reader total as they pay a bill or the perso who forgets the point separating dollars and cents on a check.

On a far bigger scale, a London trader in 2012 got his cutting and pasting *wrong* when entering figures on a computer. These seemingly **SMALL ERRORS** cost his company, J.P. Morgan, a cool $6.2 billion!

In 2013, James Howells from Wales threw away his old computer hard disk drive. Not a biggie, you'd think. YOU'D THINK. It contained 7,500 Bitcoins which, by the end of 2020, were worth over $215 million. That's gotta hurt.

These are not the only **money mistakes** made, of course. People's greed or gullibility have led them to fall for some crazy scams and hoaxes.

In 1995, Emmanuel Nwude managed to sell an airport in Nigeria he didn't own to a Brazilian bank, pocketing a commission of US$10 million. Seventy years earlier, con artist Victor Lustig sold Paris's pride and joy, the Eiffel Tower, to scrap metal dealers… not once, but twice!

You may not be offered the Eiffel Tower or a Nigerian airport, but beware any deals that sound too good to be true. Do plenty of research before you open your wallet and wave your money goodbye.

MONEY QUIZ

So you've learned all about money from cows and cowry shells to cryptocurrencies. Can you cash in and answer these challenging questions?

1. Which country issued and used banknotes long before any other?

2. In what empire would you have found a silver coin called a denarius?

3. What four-letter word describes a place where coins are produced?

4. Somalia's one-dollar coins, minted in 2004, were in the shape of which musical instrument?

5. Which country issued a 100 million billion pengő banknote in 1946?

6. What two metals are found in coins made of electrum?

7. On which Pacific island was giant stone money used: Yap, Palau, or Tahiti?

8. How much was a "horse blanket" worth in 1860s USA?

9. What kind of loans does the Grameen Bank make: megaloans, microloans, or macroloans?

10. What was the value of the first ever plastic banknote, issued by Australia?

11. What word, beginning with "c," describes interest paid on interest and the loaned sum?

12. Which world-famous scientist became warden of Britain's Royal Mint in 1696?

13. In what year were euro banknotes and coins first used as currency?

14. Which vegetable would you find on the back of a tetradrachm coin from the ancient Greek city of Selinunte?

15. How many US cents does it cost to make a one US dollar bill:
a) 3.3   b) 5.5   c) 7.7   d) 9.9

16. Can you name the currency Portugal used before it changed to the euro?

17. What two items were bought in 2010, making them the first real-world purchase using Bitcoins?

18. Mongolia's 500-tugrik coin played a speech from which US president?

7. Yap

6. Gold and silver

5. Hungary

4. An electric guitar

3. Mint

2. Roman Empire

1. China

13. 2002

12. Sir Isaac Newton

11. Compound (interest)

10. Ten dollars

9. Microloans

8. One dollar

18. John F Kennedy

17. Pizzas

16. Escudo

15. c) 7.7

14. Celery

TAKING THINGS FURTHER

Want to know more about money? Can't blame you. Here are some great guides as well as websites and videos to start your journey.

BOOKS

Money for Beginners—Eddie Reynolds, Matthew Oldham, Laura Bryan (Usborne, 2019)
Thorough guide to the world of money from its history to how banks work.

All About Money—Alvin Hall (DK, 2015)
A visual guide to money, how it has developed, and how it is used.

The Story of Money—Martin Jenkins (Walker Books, 2015)
An illustrated chapter book taking you through barter, banknotes, and banking.

Everything Money—Kathy Furgang (National Geographic, 2013)
A collection of fun facts and stories about money, including coins and banknote collecting.

Cash, Savings and All That Stuff—Kira Vermond (Franklin Watts, 2014)
Master your own money with this book on budgets, saving, and other money matters.

Dosh: How to Earn It, Save It, Spend It, Grow It, Give It—Rashmi Sirdeshpande (Wren & Rook, 2020)
Tips and tricks for money management, from entrepreneurship to shopping.

FOR OLDER READERS

How Money Works (DK, 2017)
A visual, infographics-based guide to the world of money, finance, and the economy.

WEBSITES

https://www.royalmint.com/the-royal-mint-experience/explore-the-exhibition/coins-around-the-world/
Take a tour around the world in 80 coins with this fun interactive map.

https://www.youtube.com/watch?v=IOeVvyiXxB0
Credit and debit are explored in this fascinating video, one of a series of four money videos from the British Museum.

https://thekidshouldseethis.com/post/coins-royal-mint
An entertaining video showing how modern coins are designed and minted.

https://tinyurl.com/yap27a8v
The first of seven entertaining short cartoons about the Bank of England and how it works.

https://www.youtube.com/watch?v=YCN2aTlocOw
The history of banknotes covered in this animated offering from the Open University.

https://www.youtube.com/watch?v=SzAuB2FG79A
Cryptocurrencies explained in under three minutes, courtesy of BBC News.

https://banknotes.rba.gov.au/counterfeit-detection/security-features-overview/
Watch many of the security features of banknotes in action with downloadable details.

https://www.bankofengland.co.uk/monetary-policy/inflation/inflation-calculator
See price changes over the past 800 years with this simple inflation calculator.

GLOSSARY

ASSET An object of value that a person or business owns, such as money, property, vehicles, or other things of worth.

BARTERING Swapping one thing for something else without using money.

CIRCULATION The amount of banknotes and coins issued by a country and available for use by people.

COMPOUND INTEREST Where interest is calculated on both the amount borrowed and any previous interest.

CONTACTLESS PAYMENT To make a payment quickly using a card, badge, or smartphone that can be scanned by a payment machine, without having to enter a personal code number.

COUNTERFEITING The criminal act of making fake coins and banknotes.

CREDIT The practice of obtaining goods and services now and paying for them later.

CRYPTOCURRENCY Internet-based money that is made and stored online using math and code-making techniques.

DEBT A sum of money that is owed to another person or organization, usually due to borrowing.

DENOMINATION The amount of money that a particular coin or banknote is said to be worth. It is usually printed or stamped onto the money.

ECONOMY The system of money, industry, trade, and buying and selling in a given region.

EXCHANGE RATE The amount of one currency needed to buy another currency.

GDP Short for "gross domestic product," this measures the amount of money produced by a country over a set period of time such as a year.

INFLATION When prices go up on average in a country. It is often measured as a continuous rise in the price of everyday goods.

INTEREST A sum paid for the use of money borrowed. Banks pay savers a small amount of interest.

INVESTMENT Something that is bought hoping it will generate income or be more valuable in the future.

LOAN A sum of money that has to be paid back, usually with additional money as interest.

MINT A facility that produces coins.

RECESSION A period of time when economic activity drops and a country's economy shrinks, often accompanied by job losses and rising debts.

RISK The chance that you will lose money on an investment.

SHARES A slice or portion of the ownership of a company. Most companies are divided up into thousands or millions of shares. These rise and fall in value depending on how well the company is doing.

STOCK MARKET A place where stocks and shares are bought and sold.

TRANSACTION An exchange of money or an asset between a buyer and seller.

ZERO INTEREST When a loan is made and the borrower only has to pay back the exact sum loaned.

INDEX

ALSO AVAILABLE IN THE SERIES

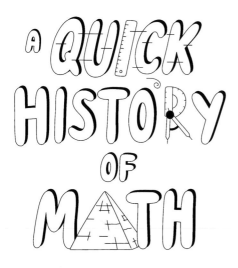

This rip-roaring rundown of the whole **HISTORY OF MATH** takes us from counting cavemen to today's big data wizards using math to solve crimes, checking out how math has changed and changed the world along the way.

From the beginning of **TIME** itself, to the formation of **STARS** and **PLANETS** and even the **EVOLUTION** of human beings, this joke-packed intergalactic history will get you up to speed on the last 13.8 billion years.

How did **ANCIENT PEOPLE** make decisions? How can you spot **FAKE NEWS**? Why did **KARL MARX** have to go without trousers? This book answers these questions and more, on a ride through time from plutocrats to people power.

CLIVE GIFFORD is an award-winning author of books for children and young adults including *Around the World in Numbers*, *Sustainable Development* and *How the World Works*. A contributor to Encyclopedia Britannica, his books have won awards from the Royal Society, Blue Peter, PBS, Smithsonian, and School Library Association.
Clive lives in Manchester, UK.

A Quick History of Money © 2021 Quarto Publishing plc.
Text © 2021 Clive Gifford
Illustrations © 2021 Rob Flowers
First published in 2021 by Wide Eyed Editions, an imprint of The Quarto Group.
100 Cummings Center, Suite 265D, Beverly, MA 01915, USA.
T +1 978-282-9590 F +1 078-283-2742 **www.QuartoKnows.com**

A CIP record for this book is available from the Library of Congress.
ISBN 978-0-7112-6275-1
eISBN 978-0-7112-6436-6
The illustrations were created artwork created with digital media
Set in Futura

Published by Georgia Amson-Bradshaw
Designed by Myrto Dimitrakoulia
Edited by Alex Hithersay
Production by Dawn Cameron

Manufactured in Guangdong, China TT112021

3 5 7 9 8 6 4 2

MIX
Paper from responsible sources
FSC® C016973